uman

The Essays

First published in Italy
in 2010 by
Skira Editore S.p.A.
Palazzo Casati Stampa
via Torino 61
20123 Milano
Italy
www.skira.net

© 2010 Uman
© 2010 Skira editore

Printed and bound in Italy.
First edition

ISBN: 978-88-572-0722-3

Distributed in North America
by Rizzoli International Publications,
Inc., 300 Park Avenue South,
New York, NY 10010, USA.
Distributed elsewhere in the world
by Thames and Hudson Ltd.,
181A High Holborn, London WC1V 7QX,
United Kingdom.

Nick Foulkes

cuba libre

elegance under the sun

SKIRA

Both of the truly memorable transactions I have conducted in Havana have been with men named Nelson and they have involved two of Cuba's most emblematic exports: **hand-rolled cigars and the straight-hemmed, open-necked over-shirt known as the 'guayabera.'**

At the time of my first visit in the mid-1990s Cuba was just emerging from what was euphemistically known as the 'special period'; a time of hardship and shortages following the collapse of the Soviet Union, when the island had yet to acquire the status of a popular tourist destination.

I was strolling along the Malecón, the broad, gracious and crumbling promenade overlooking the Straits of Florida; a few dozen shark infested miles of water separating Cuba from the fleshpots of Florida.

At the time overseas visitors were a rarity
and naive I believed the young man who
stopped me and asked to practise a few
phrases of English. These phrases quickly
coalesced around the intention of selling
me cigars and with immense skill he
extracted an order for three boxes.
This clandestine transaction was
conducted later that day, outside the
Hotel Nacional de Cuba and such was
Nelson's good nature that he even offered
to throw in a girl. I demurred, and
mistaking my reticence for a bargaining
tactic, he said that as a valued customer,
an evening with this charming chica
would be his gift to me...

A couple of years later I encountered
another Nelson, who according
to his business card styled himself
'Diseñador de Modas.' I was immediately
impressed by Nelson, it is difficult not
to respect a man who manages to put six

different typefaces on his business card, moreover he was wearing quite the most elaborate guayabera I have ever seen.
I still treasure the guayaberas I bought from him and over years of wear they have shaped my understanding of this fine, traditional Cuban garment, which is as much a receptacle of Cuban patriotism as it is a garment.

The basic architecture of the guayabera is as follows: a collar with a neckband; a yoke, sometimes fancy and evocative of 'western' shirts with decorative buttons at the various points; lines of pleats, embroidery or other embellishing stitching running the length of either side of the shirtfront and down the back; four pockets which will feature the same decorative stitching

and are once again likely to
be decorated with buttons; slits
approximately 20 cm deep
at the bottom of each sideseam
which can be closed with a
functioning buttonhole; full-
length sleeves; and of course
the defining characteristic,
the straight cut tails intended
to be worn outside the trousers,
covering the seat and ending at
the top of the thigh.
Short-sleeved versions of
guayaberas are available,
however the purist will always
choose the full-length sleeves.
To maintain its statement as
a garment that peddles that
apparent oxymoron: formal
informality, certain conventions
have to be observed. Dilute
these too much and, rather
like overenthusiastic genetic

engineering, the garment mutates into something different.

Thus the classic long-sleeved guayabera is the sartorial expression of what it is to be Cuban: an elegant and languid solution to the heat, if not the shortages, of Cuba. **It is as much a symbol of Cuba as cigars and rum.** This heat-defeating light linen or cotton overshirt is the sports jacket, the blazer, the business suit and the dinner jacket of Central America. **The go-anywhere garment of the tropics: equally at home at a government reception, chilled mojito in hand; or touring the campo, cigar clamped into the jaw and eyes shaded from the fierce tropical sun by a Panama hat.** And as an enthusiastic cigar smoker I have found that each of the four pockets holds around six cigars, which, with one in the mouth, arrives at a total of twenty-five, the number in a standard box.

Aside from its practicality as a way of carrying cigars, there is a smartness about the guayabera which eludes the merely untucked shirt: this is a garment conceived to be worn outside the trousers while the lines of pleats or embroidery remind the northern European wearer of the evening dress shirt. **But it is the transformational power of the shirt that is so remarkable,** much in the way that the dinner jacket improves even the least well favored of men; so infused with the national culture of Cuba is the guayabera, that it bestows a Central American ease on the wearer, carrying with it the feel of the tropics even unto the Mediterranean shores of Europe. It is difficult to wear it any further north than the Riviera, as, in addition to heat, the guayabera thrives on a relaxed sartorial culture. Nevertheless, there are social microclimates in Europe that permit the guayabera to take root – and one of these is the southern Spanish resort of Marbella.

Until the 1950s Marbella was a quiet coastal town in the relatively poor province of Andalucía, then there arrived the glamorous, energetic and imaginative polymath **Prince Alfonso von Hohenlohe**, the founder of the Marbella Club. Hohenlohe's impeccable social connections and his love of the place transformed this sunny spot into a sybaritic resort that rivals Saint-Tropez. He also spent a great deal of time in Mexico where he opened a club with Count Rudi von Schönburg.
"I spent two years with him in Mexico, setting up the Golden Key Club in

Mexico City in 1959 and 1960," recalls
Schönburg, "and when I came back
to revive the Marbella Club, putting in
a grill room, a beach club, new guest
cottages and suites, we were looking
for a style of dress that was relaxed
but not too casual. I had been very
struck during my years in Mexico with
the elegance of the guayabera, which
had of course come from Cuba. **Both
Alfonso and I were keen to
promote the plain white linen
guayabera, worn with colored
trousers, as the perfect balance
between formality and the
unique elegant simplicity of the
Marbella Club."**

The guayabera is perfect for the
meteorological and social climate of a
place like Marbella; it is a flamboyant
expression of machismo – decorative yet
masculine, and although it is associated

with a sense of elegant languor, there are clues in its construction that hint at martial beginnings. One theory as to the genesis of the side slits, which allow for ease of movement, is that they date back to the Cuban struggle for independence from imperial Spain. In the latter decades of the nineteenth century the machete was the weapon of choice of guerrillas and these side vents allowed them to unsheath their blades without getting them tangled in their shirt tails.

All this historical detail seems to indicate that guayabera is almost as old as colonial Cuba. One story dates the guayabera to the eighteenth century and the sleepy town of Sancti Spiritus on the banks of the Yayabo River (inhabitants of the area were known as Yayaberas), where local farmers adopted

this comfortable garment. As well as the Yayabo connection, another possible derivation was from the 'guaya' or 'guava,' from which many of the locals made their living.

Following the War of Independence at the end of the nineteenth century, in which future President Theodore Roosevelt participated so enthusiastically, links between Cuba and the United States of America strengthened and during the first half of the twentieth century Cuba became in effect a client state of its northerly neighbour succumbing to the Monroe Doctrine. Cuba became a playground for American tourists and by the 1930s the guayabera was entering the mix of American leisure wear. "In 1936 John Wanamaker in Philadelphia introduced a new sports shirt or jacket shirt that was called the Guayaberra,

14

1 *The Duke of Windsor wearing his interpretation of a tropical shirt-jacket at a barbecue in Havana, 1948*

2 *A 'hot' guayabera*

3 *EU's envoy Javier Solana stands next to Philippine Foreign Secretary Alberto Romulo. Both are wearing a 'Barong Tagalog,' a traditional formal Philippine shirt-jacket made of natural fibers (banana, pineapple), hand-embroidered with stiff collar and cuffs*

4 *May 2002: former US President Jimmy Carter on his historical visit to Fidel Castro in Cuba*

5 *An elegant Puerto Rican man wears a fedora hat and a guayabera shirt*

an authentic copy of the garment worn
by sugar planters in Cuba. It was made
of a fine-quality linen in a natural or
beige color and also in dark blue, dark
brown, and yellow. Its unlined collar
was made to be worn buttoned or open,
and its cuffs to be worn barrel or link
fashion; among other styling features
were side vents, a yoke, and a panel
back. It was a substantial shirt for its
$10 price tag, and soon Wanamaker
was selling trousers made of the same
material in matching or contrasting
colors. The Guayaberra maintained
its popularity and was seen in many
different fabrics and patterns throughout
the decade" ('Esquire's Encyclopaedia
of 20th Century Men's Fashion'). But,
however fond the American tourist might
have been of guayaberas, bringing them
home as souvenirs or wearing them on
the golf courses back home, it appears
that this rural antecedence tainted the

garment somewhat for the more prim members of the mid-twentieth-century Cuban elite. **In 1948 a series of talks on guayabera were given at the highly correct sounding Lyceum Lawn Tennis Club of Havana, which dealt with an alarming social problem known as 'guayaberismo.'** These talks were collected together into a remarkable book called the 'Use and Abuse of the Guayabera.' What exercised the members of the Lyceum Lawn Tennis Club of Havana was the pernicious decadence of the guayabera and its increasing prevalence even in polite society.

In this book, one of the authors argued that wearing a guayabera was inconsistent with appreciation of the refined pleasures of life such as gastronomy and the performing arts and he called for a six o'clock curfew on the garment, after which time it would not appear in polite society. However, he did at least respect the garment's revolutionary origins, but pointed out that circumstances had changed. "When we remember that the liberators used the guayabera as a military uniform, we can respond as well that they ate roots and wild animals, because heroism and duty submit us to any number of bothersome elements."

Another writer went even further with a quite hysterical denunciation of the guayabera and its pernicious effects on civilized existence; voicing fears of what he called a 'guayabera republic' he asked the rhetorical question "Do you know what this would signify? Simply that we renounce civilization and the culture to which we have always belonged and which we have chosen, in order to create in the future art, literature, and politics that are exclusively guayaberistic.

Or what amounts to the same: art, literature and politics without universal aims, lacking in rigor, bearing the seal of laziness, backwardness, not amounting to anything?" It was even reported that President Prio, who was elected in that same year and presided over a relatively liberal regime, until ousted by a coup from Fulgencio Batista, took the step of prohibiting the shirts on certain occasions.

This ignited a debate that gripped the nation. It seems more than slightly ridiculous that a shirt could command such attention, but then this was no ordinary shirt. A contemporary survey demonstrated that 80% of Cuban men of all backgrounds and ages wore the guayabera. Everyone from editors to intellectuals came into the debate, which is recounted at some length in an essay called 'Guayaberismo and the Essence of Cool' by Marylin Miller.

However the guayabera outlasted the Lyceum Lawn Tennis Club of Havana and contrary to what its members were told, it has enjoyed a rich tradition of involvement in literary life. Hemingway, history's most famous honorary Cuban, was a keen devotee of all things Cuban: its Daiquiris, its cigars, its fishing and its guayaberas.

Indeed in a country with such a turbulent history, in which so much has changed and where more change looks likely, the presence of the guayabera seems about the only thing it is possible to rely on. **"The loose-fitting shirts as Cuban as rum and cigars,"** commented the *Havana Journal* **in 2003.** "Fidel Castro's bodyguards often sport guayaberas, most Cuban men own at least one and the shirts remain the dress of choice for any formal occasion." **What was once restricted by presidential decree is now the default dress on occasions that require dignity and decorum.**

The shirt however achieved its apotheosis in 1994, when, attending a summit in Colombia Castro softened his traditional military attire with the addition of a guayabera. Of this combination of military and civilian dress, he commented: "My guayabera and my uniform, however, are the Latin American of which Bolivar and Martí dreamt. As I said today to our friends, we are not worthy of speaking about Martí and Bolivar until we attain a united, politically and economically, integrated Latin America. This is my dream, and I believe, the dream of every progressive and revolutionary man of Latin America."

It is eloquent testimony to the cultural weight of the guayabera that Castro was able to use it as a metaphor for the spread of revolutionary ideas in Spain's quondam colonies and as a way of invoking of the great revolutionaries Simon Bolivar and José Martí. The irony was that, when he attended this Latin American summit, the Cuban leader did not have a guayabera and was only wearing one at the request of the conference organizers. "What happened, as I explained today to our friends, is that we were all asked to make an effort to show up in short sleeves and guayaberas because of the heat. To tell you the truth, I did not have a single guayabera. I had to borrow some and try them on to see if they would fit, but none did. They made some guayaberas for me in a few hours. First, they had to find the fabric. We did

not have any fabric. They were trying
to make a green guayabera, but we could
not find the fabric anywhere. They tried
a strong blue hue, but the only fabric
that the people who do this for the
Council of State and institutions, that
outfit people when they have to fulfill
a function, had available was this clear
color. They are good at this.
They made a great effort, did not sleep.
It was chaos. I was scheduled to depart
on Monday night, and by midmorning,
they tried a guayabera on me that they
had finished at who knows what hour.
They were concerned about the length
of the sleeves, the fit of the shoulders,
and whether it needed to be a quarter-
inch longer. The first one they made was
like a dressing gown. I fit in it twice.
I said: I am really not this fat. [laughter]
They did not have my measurements
or anything. They fixed it. I am pleased.
It came out quite well." And as these

shirtmakers sewed they probably did not know that they were stitching together the fabric of history, as Castro put it, "this guayabera made history. Many praised it. Some people were against it."

Although at the time he said much about not abandoning his trademark olive green uniform, the guayabera seemed to have woven its enchantment around him. He would later continue to articulate the revolutionary struggle through his shirt, most notably appearing once alongside a similarly 'enguayaberado' Jimmy Carter, on the latter's historic visit to Cuba in 2002, the first American President, albeit not a serving one, to visit Cuba since Castro toppled the hated Batista in 1959.

In fact so significant is the cultural legacy of the guayabera that President Castro is not the only politician who has used its power to achieve a political effect. Given the large exiled Cuban Community in Miami, it has a rather different meaning to the revolutionary one that Castro imputed. **In January 2008, Mitt Romney appeared in a white guayabera to address Cuban-Americans in Miami:** "It's an honor to be able to wear this guayabera today," he said of the shirt that had been presented to him at the Bay of Pigs Museum and Library in Miami by Luis Arrizurieta, a veteran of the US-backed abortive invasion attempt of April 1961. It was noted that Romney looked less than comfortable in the shirt: "I have a feeling I won't be wearing it throughout the campaign," he said. "But I sure am proud of wearing it on such a warm day in Miami."

The picture of a slightly ill-at-ease Romney in a guayabera seems to be the answer to a question posed by the *Miami Herald* in August of the preceding year, when it asked **"Has the guayabera finally crossed over?" Although what the paper was identifying was not the guayabera's adoption by right wingers hoping to find favor with the Cuban American lobby, but rather its espousal by a young and affluent crowd.** Traditionally the guayabera as worn in Miami was a feature of the exiled Cuban Community and over the years it has become a style signature of the city. **As far back as 1993, the Metro Commission spelled it out for the rest of the population by unanimously proclaiming June, July and August 'official**

guayabera months' permitting local government employees to wear guayaberas during the steamy summers.
While La Casa de las Guayaberas, on Miami's Calle Ocho, run for decades by émigré Cuban Ramon Puig the 'King of the Guayabera,' is an established tourist attraction. However the article, which identified Florida's traditional guayabera wearers as "rather aged gentlemen of indifferent means who divide their lives between idealizing the island and cursing Fidel Castro," detected a shift in the way it was being worn and how it had its appeal had moved beyond nostalgic exiles, tourists and civil servants.

At the opening of Andy García's 'Rum Bar at the Key Biscayne Ritz-Carlton Resort' journalist Enrique Fernández had noticed that "the crowd was

filled with men in guayaberas. Yes it was a Cuba-themed evening, but the guayaberas were not a costume; for one they looked too expensive. The men wearing them were the kind who could afford anything."

And there is a brisk business to be done in bespoke guayaberas: with personal touches running from the simple monogram to such practical modifications as lines of stitching running the length of the upper pockets, creating divisions for cigars, pens and sunglasses and the formal notes like a double cuff fastened by cufflinks.

Given the immense symbolic importance it holds for Cubans, both on and off the island, it is therefore slightly ironic that there is a longstanding doubt about exactly where the guayabera originated.

On June 30, 2004 the *Miami Herald* ran an article about the guayabera under the headline 'Guayabera's Origin Remains a Puzzle.' The article, running on the eve of 'Guayabera Day' (July 1 being the birthday of the nineteenth-century Cuban poet and celebrant of rural life, Juan Cristóbal Napoles Fajardo or 'El Cucalambe' who wrote a poem about the guayabera as a Cuban symbol), explained how different Central American nations wanted to claim the Guayabera as their own. Its use in recent decades by high-profile heads of state such as Hugo Chávez as well as cultural leaders of the stature of Colombian writer Gabriel García Márquez, who wore one when collecting his Nobel Prize in 1982, shows how it is increasingly representative of the region rather than one country. However, the most serious rival to Cuba as the birthplace of the guayabera is Mexico.

There is a school of thought that teaches that the guayabera in fact originated on the Yucatán Peninsula and it is sometimes known by the sobriquet 'Mexican Wedding Shirt.' Certainly the guayabera's use in Mexico goes well beyond merely matrimonial, having been worn by presidents Alvárez and Vicente Fox in the transaction of their presidential duties. And the popularity of the shirt in Mexico, along with the country's notoriously porous border with America has led to a flourishing guayabera tradition in parts of New Mexico and Texas. **At times the guayaberas made in America's southern states are so good that people in Mexico will cross the border for them.**

In a sequence of events that neatly encapsulates the complex and multi-layered cultural history of the guayabera, it was while in Havana on a recent visit that I was introduced to the work of Dos Carolinas, a niche brand selling high-quality linen guayaberas as well as making them bespoke. Dos Carolinas is based in San Antonio, Texas and the man who was wearing their guayaberas was the distributor for Cuban cigars in Mexico.

François Berthoud
*Born in Switzerland,
1961, lives and works in
Zurich. He is known for
his fashion illustrations.
Since the mid-1980s,
François Berthoud has
been mainly engaged
in artistic activities.
His high-impact images
bring art, fashion
and communication
together. He has
published books, staged
exhibitions and realized
special fashion projects.
He is a contributor
to major magazines
worldwide.*

Nick Foulkes
*is the critically
acclaimed author
of 'Dancing into
Battle: A Social
History of the Battle
of Waterloo' and
at least a dozen
other books
on subjects as
diverse as the history
of the trench coat
and American high
society. In 2007
he was named
Havana Man of the
Year. In Debrett's
his leisure interests
are listed as playing
backgammon and
visiting watch and
cigar factories.*

*The publisher would like to thank the
following for the use of their photographs
in this publication, pp. 14–15:
1. Private Collection
2. Spike Mafford / Getty Images
3. Francis Malasig / EPA / Corbis
4. Associated Press – Lapresse
5. Tony Arruza / Corbis*

Picture research by Lynda Marshall

**cover and back cover image
by François Berthoud**